Index

pages

Published by Ordnance Survey of Northern Ireland.™
The contents of this publication cannot be copied in whole or in part without the written permission of Copyright Section, Ordnance Survey of Northern Ireland, Colby House, Stranmillis Court, Belfast BT9 5BJ. © Crown Copyright 2002

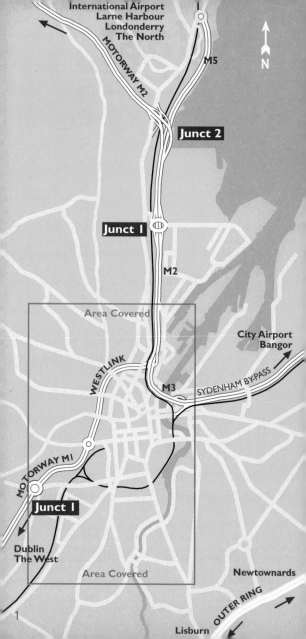

Legend

Art Gallery	
Building of Interest	
Church	
Cinema	
Concert Hall, Theatre	
Hotel	
Leisure Centre	
Museum	
National Cycle Network	
Public Car Park	
Public Telephone	
Railway / Bus Station	
Adjoining Map Number	

Scale 1:7000

Each map is one Kilometre or 0·6 of a mile Square

MAP 1

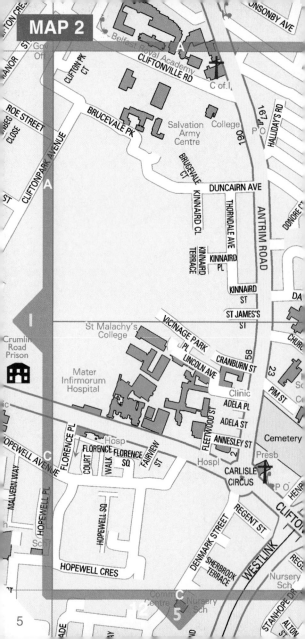

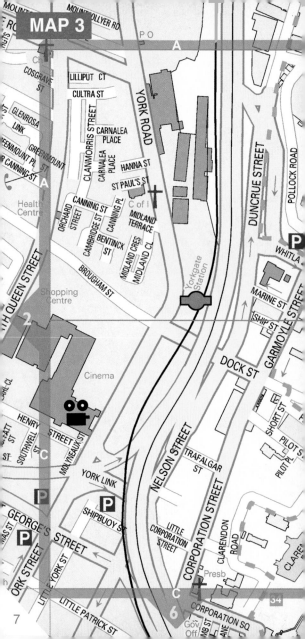

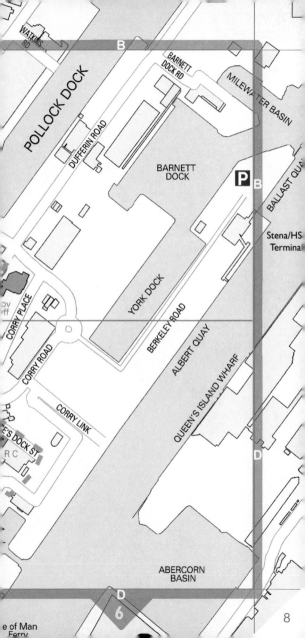

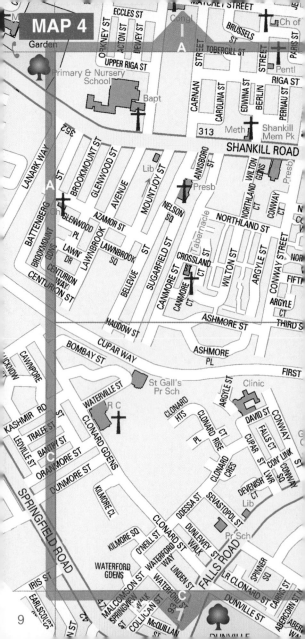

MAP 4

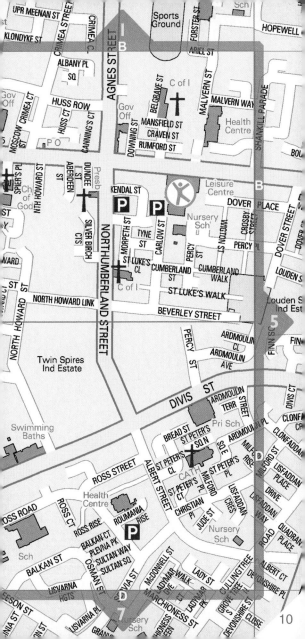

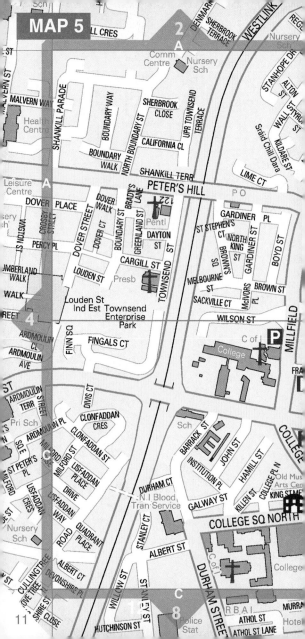

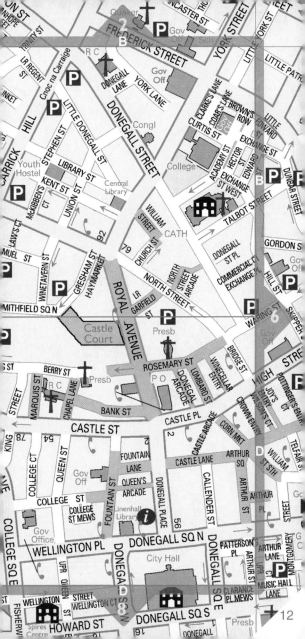

ABERCORN
BASIN

3
B

Isle of Man
Ferry
Terminal

Odyssey
Centre

B

P

QUEEN'S QUAY

SCRABO ST

STATION ST FLYOVER

STATION ST

MIDDLEPATH ST

39

48

DALTON ST

P

P

BRIDGE END

P

STRA

S

15

LOUGH LEA

ROTTERDAM ST

ROTTERDAM CT

GREGGS QUAY

LAGANVIEW MEWS

LAGANVIEW COURT

D

LAGANSIDE WALKWAY

SHORT STRAND

Waterfront Hall

RIVER LAGAN

CLYDE CT

Hotel

D

LAGANBANK RD

ALBERT
BRIDGE

D
9

BRIDGE STREET

MAYS MEADOWS

14

MAP 7

WATERFORD GDENS

IRIS ST

WATERFORD WAY

WATERFORD ST

LAUREL ST

SPINNER SQ

LR CLONARD ST

CAIRNS ST

EARLSCOURT ST

HARROWGATE ST

IRIS ST

MALCOMSON ST

SPRINGVIEW WALK

COLLIGAN ST

McQUILLAN ST

DUNVILLE ST

ABERCORN WALK

HAWTHORN ST

CROCUS ST

VIOLET ST

CAVENDISH SQ

DUNVILLE PARK

SORELLA ST

LINCO

CAVENDISH ST

St Paul's Pri Sch

R C

Royal Victoria Hospital

A

Pr Sch

St Dominic's Grammar Sch

Maternity Hospital

THAMES ST

BRAENAR ST

THAMES CT

IRWELL CT

P

Children's Hospital

P

WESTLINK

MILNER ST

EMPIRE PDE

EMPIRE STREET

RYDALMERE

BROADWAY

C

Broadway Industrial Estate

LEMBER STREET

MONARCH PDE

MONARCH ST

ROCKLAND ST

451

LR ROCKVIEW ST

LR KILBURN ST

MERIDI ST

MALDON ST

Prim Sch

Meth

STREET

P.O

C of I

NUBIA ST

306

15

STREET

LE STREET

ENBURB

NAGH

EW STREET

C 10

STREET

PARADE

STREET

KITCHENER DRIV

BROADWAY

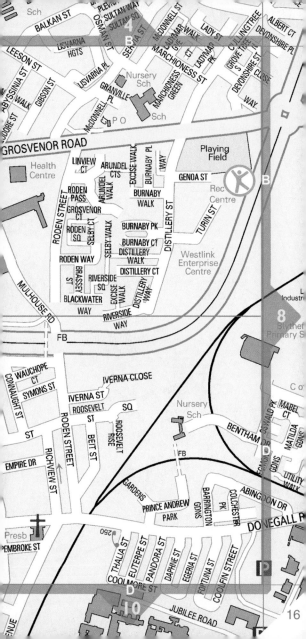

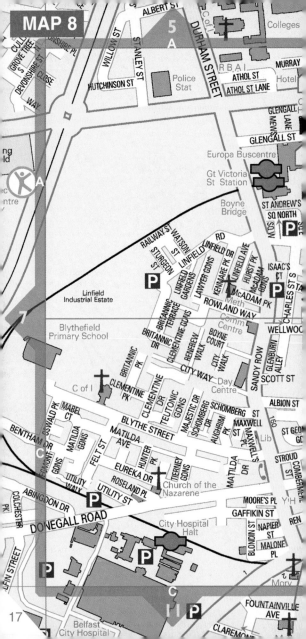

MAP 8

ALBERT ST

5A

C of I

DURHAM STREET

Colleges

MURRAY

WILLOW ST

STANLEY ST

DEVONSHIRE PL

CULL

GROVE TREE

DEVONSHIRE CLOSE

WAY

HUTCHINSON ST

Police Stat

R B A I

ATHOL ST

ATHOL ST LANE

Hotel

ng ld

GLENGALL MEWS

LANE

GLENGALL ST

A

C centre

ntre

Europa Buscentre

Gt Victoria St Station

Boyne Bridge

ST ANDREW'S

SQ NORTH

SQ

P

RAILWAY ST

WATSON ST

STURGEON ST

RD

LINFIELD

LINFIELD DR

LINFIELD AVE

HURST PK

ISAAC'S CT

ST

LINFIELD GARDENS

LINFIELD GDNS

LAWYER GDNS

KENMARE PK

McADAM PK

P

CHARLES ST

7

Linfield Industrial Estate

P

BRITANNIC TERRACE

CLEMENTINE GDNS

Meth

Comm Centre

McADAM PK

ROWLAND WAY

WELLWOO

Blythefield Primary School

BRITANNIC DR

RENFREW WALK

BOYNE COURT

CITY WALK

Day Centre

CITY WAY

SANDY ROW

GLENBURN ALLEY

SCOTT ST

C of I

BRITANNIC PK

CLEMENTINE PK

CLEMENTINE DR

TEUTONIC GDNS

SCHOMBERG DR

SCHOMBERG ST

ALBION ST

ST GEO GC

MABEL CT

OSWALD PK

MATILDA GDNS

BLYTHE STREET

MAJESTIC DR

SCHOMBERG

AUGHRIM

MAXWELL ST

MAXWELL'S

BENTHAM DR

EGMONT GDNS

MATILDA AVE

FELT ST

HUNTER PK

TIERNEY GDNS

ST

STROUD

COMBER

C

ABINGDON DR

UTILITY WALK

EUREKA DR

ROSELAND PL

UTILITY ST

Church of the Nazarene

MATILDA DR

C

P

MOORE'S PL

YH

COLCHESTER PK

DONEGALL ROAD

City Hospital Halt

GAFFIKIN ST

BLONDIN ST

NAPIER ST

MALONE PL

REN

LFIN STREET

P

P

P

C

Mory

FOUNTAINVILLE AVE

17

Belfast City Hospital

P

CLAREMON

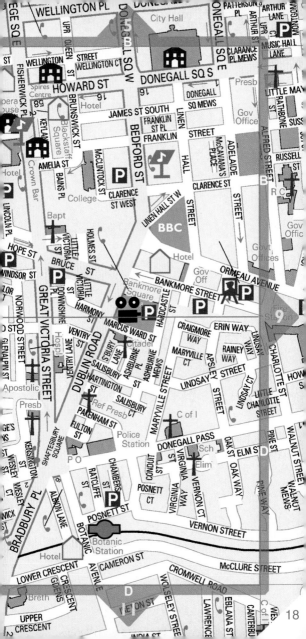

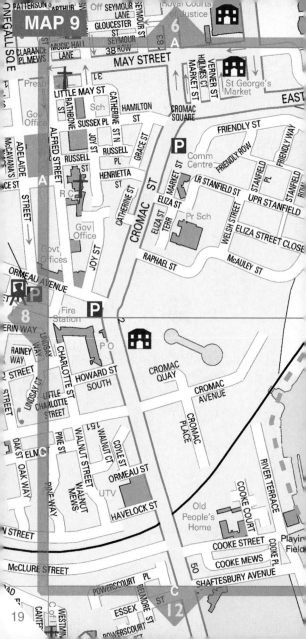

MAP 9

PATTERSON S
ARTHUR
Off SEYMOUR LANE
SEYMOUR
GLOUCESTER
ST
SEYMOUR
38 ROW
Royal Courts Justice
6A

CLARANCE
PL MEWS
MUSIC HALL
LANE
'83

DONEGALL SQE

MAY STREET

Presb

Gov't
Office

LITTLE MAY ST
RATHBONE ST
Sch
HAMILTON
ST
CROMAC
SQUARE

VERNER ST
HOLMES CT
MARKET ST
St George's
Market
EAST

McCAVANA'S
ADELAIDE
STREET
ALFRED STREET
CATHERINE ST N
SUSSEX PL
JOY ST
RUSSELL
ST
RUSSELL
PL
HENRIETTA
GRACE ST

FRIENDLY ST
Comm
Centre
FRIENDLY ROW
FRIENDLY WAY

P

MARKET ST
LR STANFIELD ST
STANFIELD PL
STANFIELD ROW

CE ST

R C

CATHERINE ST
CROMAC ST
ELIZA ST
ELIZA ST TERR
Pr Sch
UPR STANFIELD
WELSH STREET
ELIZA STREET CLOSE

Gov't
Office

JOY ST
RAPHAEL ST
McAULEY ST

ORMEAU AVENUE

P

8

Fire
Station
P
PO

ERIN WAY
RAINEY WAY
LINDSAY WAY
CHARLOTTE ST

CROMAC QUAY

CROMAC
AVENUE

RAINEY
STREET
LINDSAY WAY
HOWARD ST
SOUTH

LITTLE
CHARLOTTE
STREET

P O

CROMAC
PLACE

STREET

OAK ST
ELM C
OAK WAY

PINE ST
PINE-WAY
WALNUT STREET
WALNUT
MEWS
WALNUT CT
151
COYLE ST
ORMEAU ST
UTV
HAVELOCK ST

RIVER TERRACE

COOKE COURT

Old
People's
Home

N STREET

McCLURE STREET
POWERSCOURT PL
BELMORE ST
ESSEX ST

C of I
WESTM

COOKE STREET
COOKE MEWS
SHAFTESBURY AVENUE
50
COOKE PL

Playin
Field

19
CANTF

C
12

POWERSCOURT

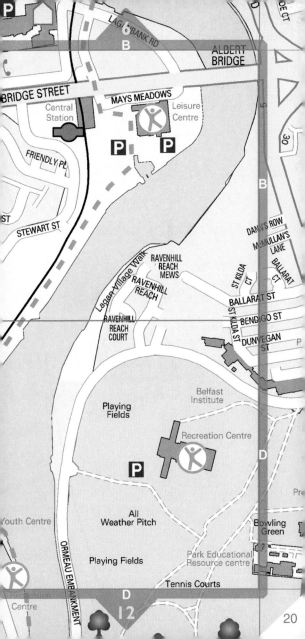

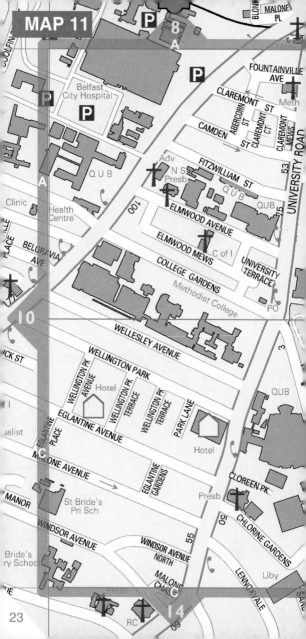

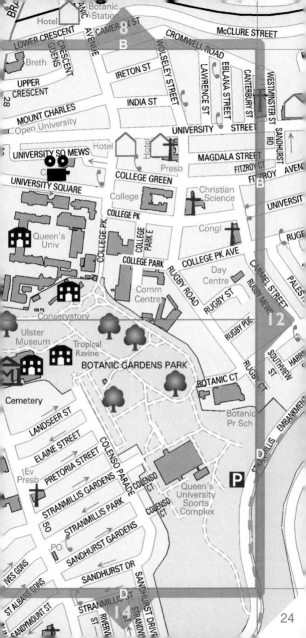

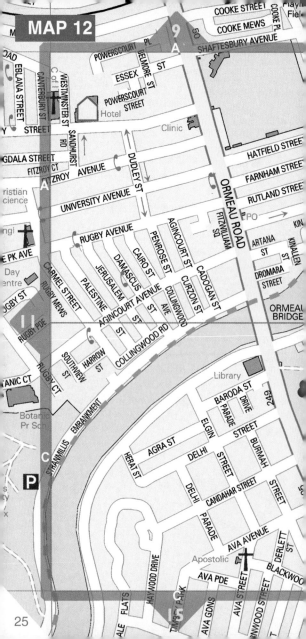

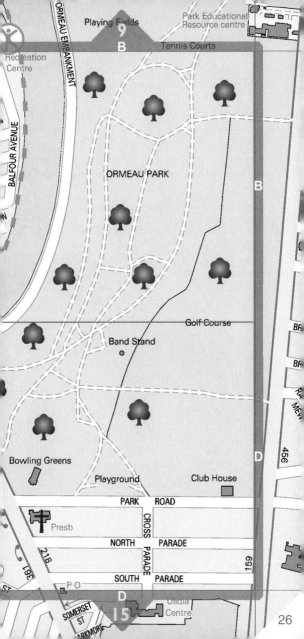

Playing Fields

Park Educational
Resource centre

Tennis Courts

Recreation
Centre

ORMEAU EMBANKMENT

BALFOUR AVENUE

ORMEAU PARK

B

Golf Course

Band Stand

BR

BR

MEV

456

D

Bowling Greens

Playground

Club House

PARK   ROAD

Presb

CROSS   PARADE

NORTH   PARADE

218

159

361

SOUTH   PARADE

P O

D

Ulidia
Centre

SOMERSET
ST

RKMORE

MAP 13

SURREY STREET
ETHEL STREET
GREAT N
Adelade
Industrial Estate
WILDFLOWER WAY
10 A
FB
Adelaide Halt
LISBURN AVE
ADELAIDE AVE
BROOKLAND ST
RATHCOOL ST
RATHDRUM ST
C of I
RATHGAR ST
FALCON ROAD
509
LISBURN RO
Evang
Presb Ch
Po
S
FERNDALE ST
MARLBOROUGH COURT
MARLBOROUGH AVE
FERNDALE PLACE
MARLBOROUGH CT
MAYFIELD ST
MARYVILLE AVE
HUGH ST
PO
MARLBOROUGH PARK
346
Fire Station
Quaker Meeting House
MAR
MARLE
CHARLEVILLE AVE
Drumglass Park
MARLBO
A
BALMORAL RD
MOWHAN ST
MOONSTONE ST
CAPSTONE ST
ARKSTONE
LISLEA AVE
697
BAWNMORE CT
BAWNMORE AVE
LANCEFIELD RD
CRANMORE AVENUE
CRANMORE GARDENS
CRANMORE PAR
RANDAL PK
CRANMORE PK
C
BAWNMORE ROAD
OSBORNE PARK
OSBORNE DRIVE
Prep Sc
OSBO
MYRTLEFIELD PARK
C

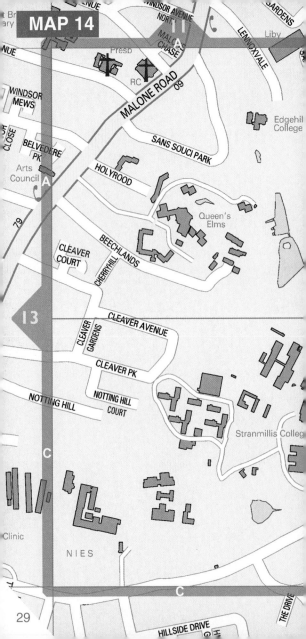

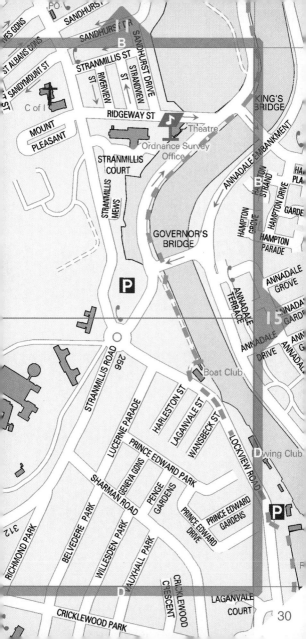

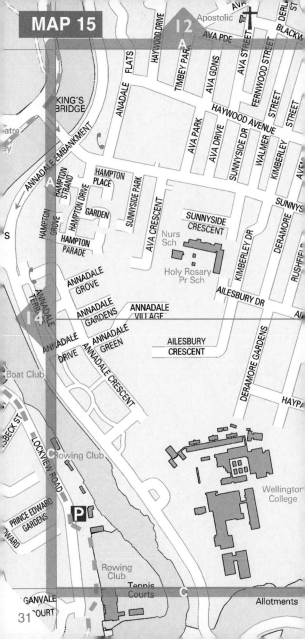

Street Location Index

Street names are listed alphabetically.
Each name has a reference number linking it to a map followed by a reference letter linking to a quadrant on that map.

eg. "Street **X** map 5B," would fall in Map **5**, Square **B**

MAP 5

A	X B
C	D

Abercorn Street	map 11A		Ailesbury Road	map 15D
Abercorn Street North	7A		Ailesbury Road	15D
Abercorn Walk	7A		Albany Place	4B
Aberdeen Street	4B		Albany Square	4B
Abingdon Drive	7D		Albert Bridge	9B
Abyssinia Street	7B		Albert Court	5C
Abyssinia Walk	7B		Albert Square	6A
Academy Street	5B		Albert Street	5C
Acton Street	1C		Albert Street	4D
Adela Place	2C		Albertville Drive	1B
Adela Street	2C		Albion Lane	8D
Adelaide Avenue	13A		Albion Street	8C
Adelaide Chase	13B		Alfred Street	9A
Adelaide Park	13B		Alloa Street	1B
Adelaide Street	8B		Alton Street	5A
Agincourt Avenue	12A		(Sráid Loch Altáin)	
Agincourt Street	12A		Ambleside Street	1C
Agnes Close	1D		Amelia Street	8B
Agnes Street	4B		Ann Street	6C
Agra Street	12C		Annadale Crescent	15C
Ailesbury Crescent	15C		Annadale Drive	15C
Ailesbury Drive	15A		Annadale Embankment	15A
Ailesbury Gardens	15D		Annadale Flats	15A

Annadale Gardens	map	15A
Annadale Green		15C
Annadale Grove		15A
Annadale Terrace		14B
Annadale Village		15A
Annalee Court		1B
Annesley Street		2C
Annsboro Street		4A
Antigua Court		1A
Antigua Street		1A
Antrim Road		2A
Apollo Road		10C
Apsley Street		8D
Ardilea Court		1A
Ardilea Street		1A
Ardmore Avenue		15D
Ardmoulin Avenue		4D
Ardmoulin Close		4D
Ardmoulin Place		4D
Ardmoulin Street		4D
Ardmoulin Terrace		4D
Argyle Court		4A
Argyle Street		4C
Argyle Street		4A
Ariel Street		4D
Arnon Street		5A
(Sráid Earnáin)		
Artana Street		12A
Arthur Street		5D
Arthur Lane		6C
Arthur Place		6C
Arthur Square		5D
Arundel Courts		7B
Arundel Walk		7B
Ashburne Mews		8D
Ashburne Place		8D
Ashleigh Manor		10D
Ashley Avenue		10B
Ashley Drive		10B
Ashley Mews		10B
Ashmore Place		4C
Ashmore Street		4A
Athol Street Lane		8A
Athol Street		8A
Aughrim Park		8C
Ava Avenue		12C
Ava Crescent		15A
Ava Drive		15A
Ava Gardens		15A
Ava Park		15A
Ava Parade		12C
Ava Street	map	15A
Avoca Street		1B
Avonbeg Close		1B
Azamor Street		4A
Bains Place		8B
Balfour Avenue		12B
Balkan Court		4D
Balkan Street		4D
Ballarat Street		9B
Ballycastle Court		1B
Ballymena Court		1B
Ballymoney Street		1B
Bandon Court		1B
Bank Street		5D
Bankmore Street		8B
Bann Court		1B
Barnett Dock Road		3B
Baroda Drive		12C
Baroda Parade		12C
Baroda Street		12C
Barrack Street		5C
Barrington Gardens		7D
Bawnmore Court		13C
Bawnmore Road		13C
Bedford Street		8B
Beechlands		14A
Beechnut Place		1B
Beechpark Street		1B
Beit Street		7D
Belgrave Street		4B
Belgravia Avenue		10B
Bell Close		1C
Bellevue Street		4A
Belmore Street		12A
Belvedere Park		14D
Benburb Street		10A
Bendigo Street		9B
Bentham Drive		7D
Bentinck Street		3A
Berkeley Road		3D
Berlin Street		4A
Berry Street		5D
Beverley Street		4B
Blackwater Way		7B
Blackwood Street		12C
Blaney Street		1D
Blondin Street		8C
Blythe Street		8C
Bombay Street		4C
Bootle Street		1C

34

Botanic Avenue	map 8D	Canmore Court	map 4A
Botanic Court	11D	Canmore Street	4A
Boundary Street	5A	Canning Place	3A
Boundary Walk	5A	Canning Street	3A
Boundary Way	5A	Canning's Court	4B
Bowness Street	1C	Canterbury Street	11B
Boyd Street	5A	Capstone Street	13C
Boyne Court	8C	Cargill Street	5A
Bradbury Place	8D	Carlisle Circus	2C
Bradford Square	6A	Carlisle Parade	2D
Brady's Lane	5A	Carlisle Road	2D
Brassey Street	7B	Carlisle Square	2D
Bread Street	4D	Carlisle Terrace	2D
Bridge End	6D	Carlisle Walk	2D
Bridge Street	5D	Carlow Street	4B
Britannic Drive	8C	Carmel Street	12A
Britannic Park	8C	Carnalea Place	3A
Britannic Terrace	8A	Carnan Street	4A
Broadway	10A	Carolan Road	15D
Broadway Parade	10A	Carolina Street	4A
Bromley Street	1C	Carrick Hill	5B
Brookland Street	13A	(Cnoc Na Carraige)	
Brookmount Street	4A	Castle Arcade	5D
Brougham Street	3A	Castle Lane	5D
Brown Street	5A	Castle Place	5D
Brown's Row	5B	Castle Street	5D
Brown's Square	5A	Catherine Street	9A
Bruce Street	8B	Catherine Street North	9A
Brucevale Court	2A	Cavendish Square	7A
Brucevale Park	2A	Centurion Street	4A
Brunswick Street	8B	Centurion Way	4A
Bruslee Way	2B	Century Street	1B
Brussels Street	1C	Chadwick Street	10C
Burmah Street	12C	Chambers Street	8D
Burnaby Court	7B	Chapel Lane	5D
Burnaby Park	7B	Charles Street South	8A
Burnaby Place	7B	Charleville Avenue	13A
Burnaby Walk	7B	Charleville Street	1D
Burnaby Way	7B	Charlotte Street	9C
		Cherryhill	14A
Cadogan Park	13B	Chichester Street	6C
Cadogan Street	12A	Chlorine Gardens	11C
Cairns Street	7A	Christian Place	4D
Cairo Street	12A	Church Lane	6C
California Close	5A	Church Street	5B
Callender Street	5D	Churchill Street	2C
Cambrai Street	1C	Churchview Court	1A
Cambridge Street	3A	City Walk	8C
Camden Street	11A	City Way	8C
Cameron Street	8D	Clanmorris Street	3A
Candahar Street	12C	Claremont Court	11A

Claremont Mews	map 11A	Collingwood Avenue	map12A
Claremont Street	11A	Collingwood Road	12C
Clarence Place Mews	8B	Combermere Street	8C
Clarence Street	8B	Commercial Court	5B
Clarence Street West	8B	Conduit Street	8D
Clarendon Road	3C	Coniston Close	1C
Clarke's Lane	5B	Connaught Street	7D
Cleaver Avenue	14C	Conway Court	4A
Cleaver Court	14A	Conway Link	4C
Cleaver Gardens	14C	Conway Square	4C
Cleaver Park	14C	Conway Street	4C
Clementine Drive	8C	Conway Street	4A
Clementine Gardens	8C	Conway Walk	4A
Clementine Park	8C	Cooke Court	9C
Clifton Park Court	2A	Cooke Mews	9C
Clifton Street	2C	Cooke Place	9C
Cliftonpark Avenue	1B	Cooke Street	9C
Cliftonville Road	2A	Coolfin Street	7D
Clonard Court	4C	Coolmore Street	7D
Clonard Crescent	4C	Corn Market	5D
Clonard Gardens	4C	Corporation Square	6A
Clonard Heights	4C	Corporation Street	3C
Clonard Place	4C	Corry Link	3D
Clonard Rise	4C	Corry Place	3B
Clonard Street	4C	Corry Road	3D
Clonfaddan Crescent	5C	Cosgrave Heights	2B
Clonfaddan Street	5C	Cosgrave Street	2B
Cloreen Park	11C	Courtrai Street	1C
Cnoc Na Carraige	5B	Coyle Street	9C
(Carrick Hill)		Craigmore Way	8D
Coar's Lane	5B	Cranburn Street	2C
Colchester Park	7D	Cranmore Avenue	13C
Colenso Court	11D	Cranmore Gardens	13C
Colenso Court	11D	Cranmore Park	13C
Colenso Parade	11D	Craven Street	4B
Cole's Alley	6C	Crescent Gardens	11B
College Gardens	11A	Crimea Close	1D
College Avenue	5C	Crimea Court	4B
College Court	5D	Crimea Street	1D
College Green	11B	Crocus Street	7A
College Park	11B	Cromac Avenue	9C
College Park East	11B	Cromac Place	9C
College Park	11B	Cromac Quay	9C
College Park	11B	Cromac Square	9A
College Park Avenue	11B	Cromac Street	9A
College Place North	5C	Cromwell Road	8D
College Square East	5D	Crosby Street	4B
College Square North	5C	Cross Parade	12D
College Street Mews	5D	Crossland Court	4A
College Street	5D	Crossland Street	4A
Colligan Street	7A	Crown Entry	5D

Crumlin Road	map 1D	Donegall Road	map 8C
Cúirt Phluincéid	5B	Donegall Square East	5D
(Plunket Court)		Donegall Square Mews	8B
Cullingtree Road	4D	Donegall Square North	5D
Cultra Street	3A	Donegall Square South	8B
Cumberland Street	4B	Donegall Square West	5D
Cumberland Walk	4B	Donegall Street Place	5B
Cupar Street Lower	4C	Donegall Street	5B
Cupar Way	4C	Donnybrook Street	10D
Curtis Street	5B	Donore Court	2A
Curzon Street	12A	Dover Place	5A
Cussick Street	10D	Dover Court	5A
Custom House Square	6A	Dover Street	5A
		Dover Walk	5A
Daisyfield Street	1D	Downing Street	4B
Dalton Street	6D	Downshire Place	8B
Damascus Street	12A	Dromara Street	12A
Danube Street	1C	Dublin Road	8D
Daphne Street	7D	Dudley Street	12A
David Street	4C	Dufferin Road	3B
Dawson Street	2B	Dunbar Link	6A
Dayton Street	5A	Dunbar Street	6A
Delhi Parade	12C	Duncairn Avenue	2A
Delhi Street	12C	Duncairn Gardens	2B
Denmark Street	2C	Duncairn Parade	2B
Deramore Avenue	15A	Duncrue Street	3A
Deramore Gardens	15C	Dundee Street	4B
Deramore Street	15B	Dunlewey Street	4C
Derlett Street	12C	Dunlewey Walk	4C
Derryvolgie Avenue	10D	Dunluce Avenue	10B
Devenish Court	4C	Dunmore Street	4C
Devonshire Close	8A	Dunvegan Street	9D
Devonshire Place	5C	Dunville Street	7A
Devonshire Street	7B	Durham Court	5C
Devonshire Way	7B	Durham Street	5C
Dewey Street	1C		
Distillery Court	7B	Earl Close	2D
Distillery Street	7B	East Bridge Street	9B
Distillery Walk	7B	Eblana Street	11B
Distillery Way	7B	Ebor Drive	10A
Divis Court	5C	Ebor Parade	10A
Divis Street	4D	Ebor Street	10A
Dock Street	3C	Ebor Street	10A
Donegal Arcade	5D	Eccles Street	1C
Donegall Avenue	10A	Edenderry Street	1C
Donegall Gardens	10A	Edinburgh Mews	10D
Donegall Lane	5B	Edinburgh Street	10D
Donegall Pass	8D	Edlingham Street	2B
Donegall Parade	10A	Edward Street	5B
Donegall Place	5D	Edwina Street	4A
Donegall Quay	6A	Egeria Street	7D

Eglantine Avenue	map	11C
Eglantine Gardens		11C
Eglantine Place		10D
Egmont Gardens		8C
Eileen Gardens		13B
Elaine Street		11D
Elgin Street		12C
Eliza Street		9A
Eliza Street Terrace		9A
Eliza Street Close		9A
Elm Street		8D
Elmwood Avenue		11A
Elmwood Mews		11A
Empire Drive		7D
Empire Parade		7C
Empire Street		7C
Erin Way		8D
Essex Street		12A
Ethel Street		10C
Eureka Drive		8C
Euterpe Street		7D
Evolina Street		2B
Exchange Place		5B
Exchange Street		6A
Exchange Street		6A
Exchange Street West		5B
Excise Walk		7B
Excise Walk		7B
Fairfax Court		1A
Fairview Street		2C
Falcon Road		13A
Falls Court		4C
Falls Road		4C
Fane Street		10B
Farnham Street		12A
Felt Street		8C
Ferndale Court		13A
Ferndale Street		13A
Ferndale Place		13A
Fernwood Street		15A
Fifth Street		4A
Fingals Court		5C
Finn Square		5C
First Street		4C
Fisherwick Place		8B
Fitzroy Avenue		12A
Fitzroy Court		11B
Fitzwilliam Avenue		15B
Fitzwilliam Square		12A
Fitzwilliam Street		11A
Flax Street	map	1A
Fleetwood Street		2C
Florence Court		2C
Florence Place		2C
Florence Square		2C
Florence Walk		2C
Florenceville Avenue		15B
Florenceville Drive		15B
Forster Street		1D
Fortuna Street		7D
Fountain Lane		5D
Fountain Street		5D
Fountainville Avenue		11A
Foyle Court		1B
Francis Street		5C
Franklin Street Place		8B
Franklin Street		8B
Frederick Street		2D
Frenchpark Street		10A
Friendly Place		9B
Friendly Row		9A
Friendly Street		9A
Friendly Way		9A
Fulton Street		8D
Gaffikin Street		8C
Galway Street		5C
Gamble Street		6A
Gardiner Place		5A
Gardiner Street		5A
Garmoyle Street		3C
Geneva Gardens		14D
Genoa Street		7B
Geoffrey Street		1C
Ghent Place		1C
Gibson Street		7B
Gipsy Street		15B
Glenalpin Street		8D
Glenburn Alley		8C
Glenfarne Street		1D
Glengall Lane		8A
Glengall Mews		8A
Glengall Street		8A
Glenhill Court		1A
Glenmachan Street		10A
Glenpark Court		1A
Glenpark Street		1A
Glenravel Street		2D
Glenrosa Link		2B
Glenrosa Street		2B
Glenrosa Street South		2B

Glentilt Street	map 1D		Haypark Gardens	map 15C
Glenview Court	1B		Haywood Avenue	15A
Glenview Street	1B		Haywood Drive	12C
Glenwood Place	4A		Hazelfield Street	1D
Glenwood Street	4A		Hector Street	5B
Gloucester Street	6C		Henrietta Street	9A
Gordon Street	6A		Henry Place	2C
Grace Street	9A		Henry Street	2D
Gracehill Court	1A		Herbert Street	1A
Granville Place	7B		Herat Street	12C
Great George's Street	2D		High Street	6C
Great Northern Street	10C		High Street Court	6A
Great Patrick Street	6A		Hill Street	6A
Great Victoria Street	8D		Hillman Street	2B
Greenland Street	5A		Hillview Court	1B
Greenmount Place	2B		Hillview Road	1A
Greenmount Street	2B		Hogarth Street	2B
Greggs Quay	6D		Holmes Court	9A
Gresham Street	5B		Holmes Street	8B
Groomsport Court	1B		Holyrood	14A
Groomsport Street	1B		Hope Street	8B
Grosvenor Court	7B		Hopewell Avenue	1D
Grosvenor Road	7B		Hopewell Crescent	2C
Grove Tree North	4D		Hopewell Place	1D
Grove Tree South	7B		Hopewell Square	2C
			Howard Street South	9C
Haddow Street	4C		Howard Street	8B
Halliday's Road	2A		Howe Street	1C
Hamill Street	5C		Hugh Street	13A
Hamilton Street	9A		Hunter Park	8C
Hampton Drive	15A		Hurst Park	8A
Hampton Garden	15A		Huss Court	4B
Hampton Grove	14B		Huss Row	4B
Hampton Parade	15A		Hutchinson Street	8A
Hampton Place	15A			
Hampton Strand	15A		Ilchester Street	2B
Hanna Street	3A		India Street	11B
Hardcastle Street	8B		Institution Place	5C
Hardinge Place	2B		Ireton Street	11B
Harleston Street	14D		Isaac's Court	8A
Harmony Street	8B		Iverna Close	7D
Harrison Walk	1C		Iverna Street	7D
Harrow Street	12C			
Harrybrook Street	1D		Jaffa Street	1D
Hartington Street	8D		James Street South	8B
Hartwell Place	2B		Jameson Street	15B
Hatfield Street	12A		Jersey Place	1C
Havelock Street	9C		Jerusalem Street	12A
Hawthorn Street	7A		John Street	5C
Haymarket	5B		Joy Street	9A
Haypark Avenue	15B		Joy Street	9A

Joy's Entry	map 6C	Lecale Street	map 10A
Jubilee Road	10B	Leeson Street	7B
Jude Street	4D	Lemberg Street	7C
		Lennoxvale	14A
Kendal Street	4B	Leopold Street	1A
Kenmare Park	8A	Lepper Street	2B
Kensington Street	8D	Library Street	5B
Kent Street	5B	Liffey Court	1B
Keswick Street	1C	Lilliput Court	3A
Keyland's Place	8B	Lime Court	5A
Kilburn Street	10A	Lincoln Avenue	2C
Kildare Street	5A	Lincoln Place	8B
(Sráid Chill Dara)		Lincoln Square	7A
Killen Street	5C	Linden Street	4C
Kilmore Close	4C	Lindsay Court	8D
Kilmore Square	4C	Lindsay Street	8D
Kilronan Street	2B	Lindsay Way	8D
Kimberley Drive	15A	Linen Hall Street West	8B
Kimberley Street	15A	Linen Hall Street	8B
Kinallen Court	12B	Linfield Avenue	8A
Kinallen Street	12A	Linfield Drive	8A
King Street Mews	5C	Linfield Gardens	8A
King Street	5D	Linfield Road	8A
Kinnaird Close	2A	Linview Court	7B
Kinnaird Place	2A	Lisburn Avenue	13A
Kinnaird Street	2A	Lisburn Road	13A
Kinnaird Terrace	2A	Lisfaddan Drive	5C
Kitchener Drive	10A	Lisfaddan Place	5C
Kitchener Street	10A	Lisfaddan Way	5C
Klondyke Street	1D	Lisfaddan Crescent	4D
		Lisvarna Heights	4D
Lady Street	4D	Lisvarna Place	7B
Ladymar Court	7B	Little Charlotte Street	9C
Ladymar Grove	4D	Little Corporation Street	3C
Ladymar Park	7B	Little Donegall Street	5B
Ladymar Walk	4D	Little Edward Street	6A
Laganbank Road	6D	Little George's Street	2D
Laganvale Street	14D	Little May Street	9A
Laganview Court	6D	Little Patrick Street	6A
Laganview Mews	6D	Little Victoria Street	8B
Lancaster Street	2D	Little Victoria Street	8B
Lancefield Road	13C	Little York Street	3C
Landscape Terrace	1D	Lockview Road	14D
Landseer Street	11D	Lombard Street	5D
Langley Street	1C	Lorne Street	10D
Lawnbrook Avenue	4A	Louden Street	5A
Lawnbrook Drive	4A	Lower Crescent	8D
Lawnbrook Square	4A	Lower Garfield Street	5B
Lawrence Street	11B	Lower Regent Street	5B
Law's Court	5B	(Sráid Ríona Íochtair)	
Lawyer Gardens	8A	Lower Windsor Avenue	10D

40

Lwr Clonard Street	map 4C		Matchet Street	map 1C
Lower Kilburn Street	7C		Matilda Avenue	8C
Lower Rockview St	7C		Matilda Drive	8C
Lower Stanfield Street	9A		Matilda Gardens	8C
Lucerne Parade	14D		Maxwell Street	8C
Ludlow Square	2B		Maxwell's Place	8C
Lyle Street	1D		May Street	9A
			Mayfair Court	1A
Mabel Court	8C		Mayfield Street	13A
Madras Street	1C		Mays Meadows	9B
Magdala Street	11B		McAdam Gardens	8A
Magee's Lane	2D		McAdam Park	8A
Majestic Drive	8C		McAuley Street	9A
Malcomson Street	7A		McCandless Street	1C
Maldon Street	7C		McCavana's Place	8B
Malone Avenue	11C		McCleery Street	2D
Malone Chase	14A		McClintock Street	8B
Malone Place	8C		McClure Street	8D
Malone Road	13B		McDonnell Court	7B
Malvern Close	1D		McDonnell Street	4D
Malvern Street	4B		McIvors Place	5A
Malvern Way	4B		McKibben's Court	5B
Malvern Way	1D		McQuillan Street	7A
Manor Court	1B		Meadowbank Place	10C
Manor Drive	1B		Meadowbank Street	10D
Manor Street	1B		Melbourne Street	5A
Manor Street	1B		Melrose Street	10D
Manor Street	1B		Meridi Street	7C
Mansfield Street	4B		Mervue Court	2B
Maralin Place	2B		Mervue Street	2B
Marchioness Green	7B		Middlepath Street	6D
Marchioness Street	7B		Midland Close	3A
Marcus Ward Street	8D		Midland Cresent	3A
Marine Street	3A		Midland Terrace	3A
Market Street	9A		Milford Place	4D
Market Street	9A		Milford Rise	4D
Marlborough Avenue	13A		Milford Street	5C
Marlborough Court	13A		Mill Street West	1C
Marlborough Gardens	13D		Millfield	5C
Marlborough Park	13A		Milner Street	7C
Marlborough Park	13D		Moffatt Street	2D
Marlborough Park Cent	13B		Moltke Street	10A
Marlborough Park-			Molyneaux Street	3C
Cross - Avenue	13D		Monarch Parade	7C
Marlborough Park North	13B		Monarch Street	7C
Marlborough Park South	13C		Montgomery Street	6C
Marlborough Street	6C		Moonstone Street	13C
Marquis Street	5D		Moore's Place	8C
Maryuile Avenue	13A		Morpeth Street	4B
Maryville Court	8D		Moscow Street	4B
Maryville Street	8D		Mount Charles	11B

Mount Pleasant	map 14B	Oranmore Street	map 4C
Mount Prospect Park	10B	Orchard Street	3A
Mountjoy Street	4A	Orkney Street	1C
Mountview Court	1B	Ormeau Avenue	8B
Mountview Street	1B	Ormeau Embankment	9D
Mowhan Street	13C	Ormeau Road	12A
Mulhouse Road	7B	Ormeau Street	9C
Murray Street	8A	Osborne Drive	13C
Musgrave Street	6C	Osborne Gardens	13D
Music Hall Court	6C	Osborne Park	13C
Music Hall Lane	9A	Osman Street	4D
		Oswald Park	8C
Napier Street	8C	Oxford Street	6C
Nelson Square	4A		
Nelson Street	3C	Pakenham Street	8D
New Lodge Place	2B	Palestine Street	12A
New Lodge Road	2B	Pandora Street	7D
Newport Court	1B	Paris Street	1C
Ninth Street	4A	Park Lane	11C
North Boundary Street	5A	Park Road	12D
North Hill Street	2D	Parkmore Street	15B
North Howard Court	4B	Parkview Court	1A
North Howard Link	4B	Patterson's Place	5D
North Howard Street	4D	Pembroke Street	7D
North Howard Walk	4B	Penge Gardens	14D
North King Street	5A	Penrose Street	12A
North Parade	12D	Percy Place	4B
North Queen Street	2B	Percy Street	4B
North Street	5B	Percy Street	4D
North Street Arcade	5B	Pernau Street	4A
Northbrook Gardens	10C	Peter's Hill	5A
Northbrook Street	10C	Pilot Place	3C
Northland Court	4A	Pilot Street	3C
Northland Street	4A	Pim Street	2C
Northumberland Street	4B	Pine Street	9C
Norwood Street	8D	Pine Way	9C
Notting Hill	14C	Pinkerton Walk	2D
Notting Hill Court	14C	Plevna Park	4D
Notting Hill Manor	13D	Plunket Court	5B
North Howard Street	4B	(Cúirt Phluincéid)	
Nubia Street	7C	Pollock Road	3A
		Portland Place	2D
Oak Street	8D	Posnett Court	8D
Oak Way	8D	Posnett Street	8D
Odessa Street	4C	Pottinger's Court	6C
Old Lodge Road	1D	Pottinger's Entry	6C
Oldpark Road	1B	Powerscourt Place	9C
Olympia Drive	10A	Powerscourt Street	12A
Olympia Parade	10A	Pretoria Street	11D
Olympia Street	10A	Primrose Street	15B
O'Neill Street	4C	Prince Andrew Gardens	7D

Sandhurst Drive	map 11D	Spamount Street	map 2B
Sandhurst Drive	14B	Spier's Place	4B
Sandhurst Gdns	11D	Spinner Square	4C
Sandhurst Road	12A	Springfield Road	4C
Sandringham Street	10D	Springview Street	7A
Sandy Row	8C	Springview Walk	7A
Sandymount Street	14B	Sráid an Bhalla	5A
Sandymount Street	14B	(Wall Street)	
Sans Souci Park	14A	Sráid Chill Dara	5A
Saunderson's Court	1A	(Kildare Street)	
Schomberg Drive	8C	Sráid Earnáin	5A
Schomberg Street	8C	(Arnon Street)	
Scott Street	8C	Sráid Loch Altáin	5A
Scrabo Street	6B	(Alton Street)	
Selby Court	7B	Sráid na Ríona	2C
Selby Walk	7B	(Regent Street)	
Servia Street	4D	Sráid Ríona Íochtir	5B
Sevastopol Street	4C	(Lower Regent Street)	
Seymour Lane	6C	Sráid Thír Eoghain	5A
Seymour Row	6C	(Tyrone Street)	
Seymour Street	6C	St Albans Gardens	14B
Shaftesbury Avenue	9C	St Andrew's Square E	8A
Shaftesbury Square	8D	St Andrew's Square N	8A
Shankill Parade	5A	St Andrew's Square W	8A
Shankill Road	4A	St Colmban's Court	1A
Shankill Terrace	5A	St Gemma's Court	1A
Shannon Court	1D	St George's Gardens	8C
Shannon Street	1B	St Ives Gardens	11D
Sharman Road	14D	St James's Street	2A
Sherbrook Close	5A	St John's Avenue	15D
Sherbrook Terrace	2C	St Jude's Avenue	15B
Sheridan Court	2B	St Jude's Crescent	15B
Sheridan Street	2B	St Jude's Parade	15B
Ship Street	3C	St Kilda Court	9B
Shipbuoy Street	3C	St Kilda Street	9D
Short Street	3C	St Luke's Close	4B
Short Strand	6D	St Luke's Walk	4B
Silver Birch Courts	4B	St Mary's Court	1C
Silvio Street	1C	St Paul's Street	3A
Skipper Street	6C	St Peter's Court	4D
Sloan Court	10C	St Peter's Close	4D
Smithfield Square North	5B	St Peter's Place	4D
Snugville Street	1D	St Peter's Square East	4D
Snugville Street	4A	St Peter's Square North	4D
Somerset Street	15B	St Stephen's Court	5A
Sorella Street	7A	Stanfield Place	9A
Soudan Street	10A	Stanfield Row	9A
South Parade	12D	Stanhope Drive	5A
Southport Court	1B	Stanhope Street	2D
Southview Street	12C	Stanley Court	5C
Southwell Street	2D	Stanley Street	8A

Station Street	map 6D	Tomb Street	map 6A
Station Street Flyover	6D	Townhall Street	6C
Steam Mill Lane	6A	Townsend Street	5A
Stephen Street	5B	Trafalgar Street	3C
Stewart Street	9B	Trainfield Street	2B
Strandview Street	14B	Trinity Street	2D
Stranmillis Court	14B	Tudor Place	1D
Stranmillis Embankment	12C	Turin Street	7B
Stranmillis Gardens	11D	Tyne Street	4B
Stranmillis Mews	14B	Tyrone Street	5A
Stranmillis Park	11D	(Sráid Thír Eoghain)	
Stranmillis Road	14D		
Stranmillis Street	14B	**U**lster Street	6A
Stratheden Street	2B	Ulsterville Avenue	10B
Stroud Street	8C	Ulsterville Drive	10B
Sturgeon Street	8A	Ulsterville Gardens	10B
Sugarfield Street	4A	Ulsterville Place	10B
Sultan Square	4D	Union Street	5B
Sultan Way	4D	University Avenue	12A
Summer Street	1B	University Road	11A
Summerhill Court	1B	University Square Mews	11B
Sunnyside Crescent	15A	University Square	11B
Sunnyside Drive	15A	University Street	11B
Sunnyside Park	15A	University Terrace	11A
Sunnyside Street	15A	Upper Canning Street	2B
Surrey Street	10C	Upper Crescent	11B
Sussex Place	9A	Upper Meadow Street	2B
Sydney Street West	1C	Upper Queen Street	5D
Symons Street	7D	Upper Riga Street	4A
Syringa Street	2B	Upper Arthur Street	5D
		Upper Charleville Street	1D
Talbot Street	5B	Upper Church Lane	6C
Tasmania Street	1D	Upper Glenfarne Street	1D
Tate's Avenue	10B	Upper Meenan Street	1D
Tate's Mews	10D	Upper Stanfield Street	9A
Tavanagh Street	10A	Upper Townsend Terrace	5A
Taylor Street	8B	Utility Street	8C
Telfair Street	6C	Utility Walk	8C
Tennent Street	1C		
Teutonic Gardens	8C	**V**auxhall Park	14D
Thalia Street	7D	Ventry Lane	8D
Theodore Street	7B	Ventry Street	8D
Third Street	4C	Verner Street	9A
Thomas Street	2D	Vernon Court	8D
Thorndale Avenue	2A	Vernon Street	8D
Thornhill Gardens	13D	Vicinage Park	2C
Thornhill Malone	13D	Vicinage Place	2C
Tierney Gardens	8C	Victoria Parade	2D
Timbey Park	15A	Victoria Square	6C
Tobergill Street	1C	Victoria Street	6C
Tomb Street	6A	Violet Street	7A

Virginia Street	map 8D		Westminster Street	map 12A
Virginia Way	8D		Whitehall Gardens	15B
Vistula Street	1C		Whitehall Mews	15B
			Whitehall Parade	15B
Wall Street	5A		Whitla Street	3A
(Sráid an Bhalla)			Wigton Street	4B
Walmer Street	15A		Willesden Park	14D
Walnut Court	9C		William Street South	6C
Walnut Mews	9C		William Street	5B
Walnut Street	9C		Willow Street	5C
Wansbeck Street	14D		Wilson Street	5A
Waring Street	6A		Wilson's Court	6C
Waterford Gardens	4C		Wilton Gardens	4A
Waterford Street	7A		Wilton Street	4A
Waterford Way	4C		Windsor Avenue	11C
Waterville Street	4C		Windsor Avenue North	11C
Watkins Road	3B		Windsor Close	13B
Watson Street	8A		Windsor Court	13B
Wauchope Court	7D		Windsor Drive	10D
Wellesley Avenue	11C		Windsor Mews	13B
Wellington Court	8B		Windsor Park	13B
Wellington Park	11C		Windsor Road	10C
Wellington Park Avenue	11C		Windsor Street	8B
Wellington Park Terrace	11C		Winecellar Entry	5D
Wellington Park Terrace	11C		Winetavern Street	5B
Wellington Place	5D		Wolseley Street	11B
Wellington Street	8B			
Wellwood Street	8C		**Y**arrow Street	1B
Welsh Street	9A		York Lane	5B
Wesley Court	8D		York Link	3C
Wesley Street	8D		York Road	3A
Westlink	7C		York Street	2D
Westlink	2C			

About BELFAST

For information on places to go and
things to do in Belfast City, call into:

The Belfast Welcome Centre (5D)

47 Donegall Place,
Belfast BT1 5AD.
Tel: (028) 9024 6609
Fax: (028) 9031 2424
Email:belfastwelcomecentre@nitic.net
Website: www.gotobelfast.com

"Big Fish"

Donegall Quay (6A)

Belfast City Hall, Donegall Square.   map (5D)

One of the finest Classical Renaissance buildings in
Europe, this Edwardian (1906) masterpiece finished in
Portland Stone is the home of Belfast City Council.
Take a tour to see the ornate dome, grand staircase
and the priceless mural of Belfast's industrial heritage
by John Luke.

Guided tours Mon-Sat. Admission Free, Please book.
Tel: (028) 9027 0456.

Belfast Public Library, Royal Avenue. (5B)
Red sandstone from Scotland gives this imposing
classical building (1890) a distinctive look in Belfast's
most architecturally important thoroughfare. It's a
welcoming place.

Open Mon-Sat. Admission Free
Tel: (028) 9024 3233.

Belfast Waterfront Hall, Lanyon Place, Laganside. (

Open daily. Belfast's award-winning £30 million flagship is a powerful symbol of the city's renaissance. Experience the panoramic views of Belfast City overlooking the River Lagan while you enjoy lunch or coffee in the Terrace Bar Restaurant. Just a short walk from Belfast City Hall, call in to pick up a free programme, choose a show or book tickets.

Box Office, tel: (028) 9033 4455.
Web: www.waterfront.co.uk.

Crown Liquor Saloon,
46 Great Victoria Street (8B)

Northern Ireland's best-known gas-lit pub. Its ornately extravagant Victorian exterior and intoxicating interior decor make it one of the National Trust's greatest treasures. To be able to summon a creamy pint and a dozen Strangford oysters to your snug with a silent signalling system is only one of its unique features. Meet upstairs in Flannagan's for the 'Historical Pub Walking Tour' - tel: 028 9268 3665 for tour times and further details.

Open daily. Admission Free Tel: (028)90279901
Web:www.belfasttelegraph.co.uk/crown.

Grand Opera House, Great Victoria Street. (8A)

Architect Frank Matcham's late Victorian masterpiece (restored 1980) is also Northern Ireland's premier theatre, bringing world-class entertainment including theatre, musicals, opera, ballet, comedy, concerts and pantomime. Don't miss a drink in the interval bar over the pavement of one of Belfast's liveliest thoroughfares. UK Winner of Barclays/TMA Most Welcoming Theatre Award.

Ticket Shop. Tel: (028) 9024 1919
Email: info@goh.co.uk Web: www.goh.co.uk.

Linenhall Library, 17 Donegall Square North. (5D)

The Linen Hall Library is a unique institution specialising in Irish politics and culture. Founded in 1788 it is the city's oldest library, but offers the visitor much more. Facilities include a new coffee house and an extended retail line of prints and gifts, all available in this superbly refurbished building.
Admission Free

Tel: (028) 9032 1707
Email: info@linenhall.com
Web: www.linenhall.com.

Old Museum Arts Centre, 7 College Sq North. (5C)

One of Ireland's leading centres for visual and performing arts, located in a Grade A listed building of architectural importance dated 1830.

Admission to exhibitions is free, and visitors are welcome to enjoy refreshments in the coffee bar.
Tel: (028) 9023 5053

Queen's University Belfast - Visitors' Centre, University Road. (11B)

Queen's, which celebrated its 150th anniversary in 1995, is one of the oldest universities in the UK. Established in Belfast in 1845 as one of the three "Queen's Colleges in Ireland," it became a fully-fledged university in 1908, adopting its present name of 'The Queen's University of Belfast'. The Visitor Centre serves as an information point, hosts a programme of exhibitions and offers guided tours, visitor information and a selection of Queen's University memorabilia in the gift shop.
Open Mon-Fri Admission Free *Citybus 70, 71, 69*

Tel: (028) 9033 5252
Email: visitors.centre@qub.ac.uk
Web: ww.qub.ac.uk/vcentre.

The Spires Centre, Wellington Street. (5D)

Built in 1905 and refurbished in 1992, the architecturally-admired building features stained glass windows. Offering superb conference and exhibition facilities in one of Belfast's most attractive buildings. Designer fashion and giftware Shopping Mall plus café on ground floor. Admission Free

Tel: (028) 9032 2284 Open Mon-Sat.

Ulster Historical Foundation, (5C)

12 College Square East. Email: enquiry@uhf.org.uk Web: www.uhf.org.uk. Non-profit organisation founded 1956 to promote interest in Irish history and genealogy, with particular reference to Ulster. UHF offers an ancestral research service, publishes books, organises conferences and lecture tours and runs a membership Guild. Admission Free

Tel: (028) 9033 2288

St George's Market, May Street. (6C)

Market open Friday with twice-monthly Saturday Farmers' Market. More than 100 years old, but looking better than ever after restoration, Belfast City Council's famous covered marketplace is open for bargains, and is also a venue for festive events. Try its new Oxford Exchange Grill Bar. Don't miss the displays of locally-caught fish and fresh produce in one section and everything from discount clothing to second-hand videos in the aptly-named Variety Market.

Tel: (028) 9027 0386

St Anne's Cathedral, Donegall Street. (5B)

An imposing Hiberno-Romanesque monument to persistence - Belfast Cathedral was partly completed and opened in the 1890s and finished nearly a century later! The awe-inspiring baptistry is by local architect WH Lynn, the angel heads of the font by Rosamund Praeger and the mosaics by Gertrude Stein.
Admission Free

Tel: (028) 9032 8332 Open Daily.

FAMILY FUN:

Belfast Superbowl, 4 Clarence Street West. (8B)

Modernised state-of-the-art entertainment business with 20 glow-in-the-dark bowling lanes. Also, American pool, various arcade machines. Efficient staff seek to ensure you have a happy time.

Tel: (028) 9033 1466
Open Mon-Sun 10am-late.

Botanic Gardens, Stranmillis Road/Botanic Ave. (11D)

This is world-class, with its great greenhouses and glorious herbaceous walkways, formal bedding and shrubberies. The restored Palm House (1852) is a masterpiece of moulded glass and wrought iron, displaying exotic trees and flowering plants. The Tropical Ravine (1889) features a humid jungle glen plus a fish pond dominated by giant waterlilies.
Admission Free *Citybus 70, 71, 69.*

Open daily until dusk.

Castle Court Shopping Centre, Royal Avenue. (5B)

Northern Ireland's largest shopping centre extends over 8.5 acres and includes multi-storey parking for 1,600 cars. It is undercover and air-conditioned with more than 70 shops and services on two levels including Debenhams, TK Maxx, Laura Ashley, The Gap, Virgin Megastore, Boots and the Discovery Store.

Tel: (028) 9023 4591.
Web: www.castlecourtshoppingcentre.com.
Open Mon-Sat, 9am-6pm (Thurs to 9pm),
Sunday 1pm-6pm.

Lagan Boat Company, 1 Donegall Quay. (6A)

Enjoy a trip along the river Lagan in the 40-seater passenger vessel, The Joyce, to see the latest developments on Belfast's revitalised waterfront. Regular daily departures; special cruises/private parties can be arranged. Located beside the Lagan Lookout.

Information line: (028) 9033 0844 or 0771 891 0423. Operates daily. Fare Payable.

The Lagan Lookout, Donegall Quay. (6A)

Range of information exhibits about the regeneration of the Laganside area. See the working of the Lagan Weir and follow the story of Belfast's development as a modern city. Have a good look at the detailing on the 'scales' and eyes of the delightful 30ft ceramic 'Big Fish' by Belfast-born sculptor John Kindness in the piazza. Open daily.

Tel: (028) 9031 5444
Email: lookout@laganside.com
Admission Charge

Odyssey Arena, Odyssey Complex, Queen's Quay. (6B

Ireland's newest and largest all-seater indoor venue i
home to the Belfast Giants Superleague Ice Hocke
Team, as well as host to many large entertainment show
and events. Close to Belfast City Centre, the Odysse
Arena is a 'must-visit' venue for everyone!
Centrelink Bus

Tel: (028) 9076 6000
Web: www.odysseyarena.com

Sheridan IMAX, Odyssey Complex, Queen's Quay. (6B

The IMAX cinema experience is phenomenal, placing th
viewer in the movie, through the sophisticated 2D and 3I
projection system. The 62ft high screen creates a movi
experience that is thrilling, educational and fun.
Centrelink Bus

Tel: (028) 9045 2515
Web: www.sheridanimax.com

"whowhatwherewhenwhy" (6B)
W5 Odyssey Complex, Abercorn Basin, Queen's Quay.

W5 is Ireland's first purpose built interactive Discover
Centre and is part of Odyssey, Northern Ireland
Landmark Millennium Project. Visitors could easily spen
an enthralling day exploring the five exciting discover
zones - Wow, Start, Go, See and Do - and will be amaze
by the spectacular Fire Tornado or have fun playing th
Laser Harp - no strings attached!

Enjoy making giant cloud rings, plus lots more. Open daily seven days a week. Wheelchair access to all floors.
Please phone for more information on admission and opening times.
Centrelink Bus

Tel: (028) 9046 7700
Web:
www.w5online.co.uk.

© whowhatwherewhenwhy

Ulster Museum, Stranmillis Road. (11D)

A truly great museum and art gallery that deserves a full day. Rich displays of archaeology, ethnography, art, history and natural sciences. The café overlooks the ancient Friar's Bush cemetery and the Gift Shop has many unusual gift items. Admission Free
Citybus 69, 70, 71

Tel: (028) 9038 3000
Web: www.ulstermuseum.org.uk. Open Daily.

We gratefully acknowledge the Belfast Visitor and Convention Bureau who supplied this visitor information and gave permission along with Belfast City Council to use the photographs on pages 47-58. We further acknowledge "whowhatwherewhenwhy"© for permission to use the photograph on page 58.

Main Bus Departure Points - Belfast City Centre

100   Centrelink to Central Station

30,31   Ormeau (via Castlereagh Rd)
32   Braniel (via Castlereagh Rd)

39   Silverstream
57   Ligoniel
61   Carr's Glen (via Cavehill Road)
63   Glencairn
73   Springmartin

35   Carr's Glen (via Cliftonville Road)
93   Carr's Glen (via Oldpark Road)

1a,1b   Newtownabbey CityExpress
7   Abbey Centre
8   Mossley
9,10,11   Carnmoney (via Whitewell Rd)
21,25   Holywood Road
26,27   Old Holywood Road
45   Roughfort
46   Roughfort/Hydepark
47,48   Ballyhenry
49,50,51   Ballyduff
64   Downview

16,17,
20,20A   Dundonald
22,23   Parliament Buildings and Stormont
76   Gilnahirk
77   Mann's Corner

(All Sunday Services depart from
Donegall Square West)

We appreciate Translink's assistance in compiling this informatio

2 Glen Road (via Whiterock Road)
3 Lenadoon (via Glen Road)
4 Ladybrook (via Falls Road)
5 Shaw's Road
0 Ardoyne & Oldpark (via West Circular Rd)
1 Turf Lodge (via Springfield Road)

78 Mount Merrion (via Ravenhill Rd)
79 Four Winds (via Ravenhill Rd
   and Newton Pk)

33 Ormeau
   (via Cregagh Road)
34 Mount Merrion
   (via Cregagh Rd)

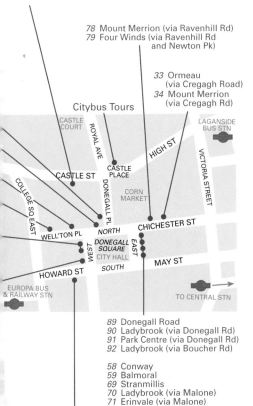

Citybus Tours

CASTLE COURT
CASTLE COURT
ROYAL AVE
HIGH ST
LAGANSIDE BUS STN
CASTLE ST
CASTLE PLACE
VICTORIA STREET
COLLEGE SQ EAST
DONEGALL PL
CORN MARKET
WELL'TON PL
NORTH
CHICHESTER ST
DONEGALL SQUARE
EAST
CITY HALL
WEST
MAY ST
HOWARD ST
SOUTH
EUROPA BUS & RAILWAY STN
TO CENTRAL STN

89 Donegall Road
90 Ladybrook (via Donegall Rd)
91 Park Centre (via Donegall Rd)
92 Ladybrook (via Boucher Rd)

58 Conway
59 Balmoral
69 Stranmillis
70 Ladybrook (via Malone)
71 Erinvale (via Malone)
95 Royal Hospital Services

82 Four Winds (via Ormeau Ave and Newton Pk)
83 Four Winds (via Botanic Ave and Newton Pk)
84 Four Winds (via Botanic Ave and Cairnshill Rd)
85 Mount Merrion (via Botanic Avenue)

(All Sunday Services depart from Donegall Square West)

Ordnance Survey of Northern Ireland would like to thank Belfast Visitor and Convention Bureau and Translink for their assistance in compiling this guide.

The mapping is based on an extract from our Belfast Street Map-2000 edition, enlarged to 1:7000 scale and updated to incorporate major change.

This product is one of a range of publications that includes large-scale and leisure mapping products.

Our leisure mapping products are available from book shops.

All our current mapping is available from our map shop at Colby House.

Ordnance Survey of Northern Ireland
Colby House,
Stranmillis Court,
Belfast BT9 5BJ,
Northern Ireland

Tel: (028) 9025 5769
Fax: (028) 9025 5735
e-mail: mapsales@osni.gov.uk
www: http://www.osni.gov.uk

Ordnance Survey of Northern Ireland is an Agency within the Department of Culture, Arts and Leisure.

Ordnance Survey
of Northern Ireland

You have enjoyed
Belfast, now explore
Northern Ireland with our
1:50 000 scale Discoverer
Series™

Discoverer Series,
Ireland North and Street
Maps are available from
bookshops or our map
shop at -
Colby House, Stranmillis
Court, Belfast BT9 5BJ
Tel 028 9025 5769